You Can Self-Publish!
A Step-by-Step Guide to Publishing and Marketing Your Book

By Cindy Freland

Copyright © 2019 by Cindy Freland

All rights reserved. No part of this publication may be reproduced, distributed, or transmitted in any form or by any means, including photocopying, recording, or other electronic or mechanical methods, without the prior written permission of the publisher, except in the case of brief quotations embodied in critical reviews and certain other noncommercial uses permitted by copyright law. For permission requests, contact the author, by email at *cindy@marylandsecretarial.com* or by phone at (301) 352-7927.

Order this book and other books written by Cindy Freland on Amazon.com.

Printed in the United States of America

Now YOU can write stories, get them published, and get paid for the books that sell.

The best part about it is it's VERY INEXPENSIVE!

It's also just plain fun, but it's also VERY INEXPENSIVE!

Kids, get your parents or an adult to help you follow the steps in this book and you will be able to write a book and publish it in no time at all.

If you don't believe it, check this out: I taught 12 middle school students how to self-publish their own books at a private school. Their books were available on Amazon within three months.

Do Not Steal!

Plagiarizing is stealing someone else's work and using it as your own. ***It is illegal!***

What is Publishing?

Publishing is repairing books to be sold to the public.

What do I write about?

Anyone can write and publish a book. All you need is a story and an Internet connection. Here are a few ideas on what to write:

1. A magical person
2. A magical place
3. A toy I want to invent
4. Being bullied
5. My favorite pet
6. My favorite things
7. My best friend
8. My family
9. My school
10. My favorite place
11. My poetry
12. Something or someone I would like to become
13. The importance of telling the truth
14. Things I don't like
15. Why am I special?
16. What I want to be when I grow up
17. What would I do if I were king or queen?
18. What would it be like to be homeless?
19. What would I do with a million dollars?

Serial Author

As of the printing of this book (March 20, 2019), I have self-published 22 books. I am working on a few more children's books. I have turned into a SERIAL AUTHOR. You can find all of my books on Amazon.com and www.cbaykidsbooks.com. There is a list of my book titles in the back of this book.

I attribute this phenomenon to my customer and friend, Ash Shukla. He has written several books about "Sell Like Crazy." He is the one who told me about Create Space. After using Create Space for a few years, I discovered Ingram Spark. This is the website I will teach you about in this book.

Too Expensive?

Have you ever wanted to write a book? But you didn't because you thought you couldn't afford it? Maybe you have information and experience that you would like to share with business owners. You might have a mystery novel or a recipe book to share with family and friends.

Well, I thought I couldn't afford it either. There are VERY INEXPENSIVE print on demand (POD) websites where you can:

- upload your formatted book
- have it available in print on Amazon
- have it available in Kindle format on Amazon
- have it available in online book stores and libraries
- get paid royalties for sales
- print as many or as few books as you like at very little cost
- sell them for profit yourself

Books are great gifts to friends and family and great giveaways to prospects and customers.

Is it Really INEXPENSIVE?

Ingram Spark (IS) is very easy to upload your book to Amazon, in print and Kindle format. The best thing about IS is that it's VERY INEXPENSIVE and you get paid ROYALTIES when your books are sold. Yes, it is really INEXPENSIVE!

There are many other POD websites so you might want to check with them before you make a decision on which one you will use for your book.

What You Will Need to Upload Your Book

- Formatted book file in Word (must be saved in PDF) include images
- Book title and subtitle
- Author and illustrator names
- Professional photo of yourself (optional)
- Image for book cover (must be saved in PDF)
- Images for inside book (may be hand-drawn and scanned in jpeg)
- Description of your book for back cover
- Description of book for Amazon
- Description of author for back cover
- ISBN
- Categories
- Genre
- Pricing

Your Account

Start by going to www.ingramspark.com and create your FREE account. **You will need your account email address and your password every time you log in so keep track of them.**

Book Cover

You will need to design the book cover yourself or get an illustrator to do it for you. If you do it yourself, you may draw your images on paper and scan them. If you do them digitally, you will already have them in your computer.

I have found most of my illustrators through Facebook author and illustrator groups. You might want to shop around for an illustrator as they can be very expensive. In my shopping, I have found some that charge as much as $1,000 an image. I enjoy paying about $60 each for mine and about $150 for the cover front and back. You may also check with www.fiverr.com as they have very inexpensive illustrators.

Book Cover Template

IS has free book cover templates. To request a free template, just click on "Help" on the left. Then click "Cover Template Generator." All you need to do is request them and they automatically calculate the size and email them to you almost immediately. You will need a different size book cover for a paperback and for a hardback.

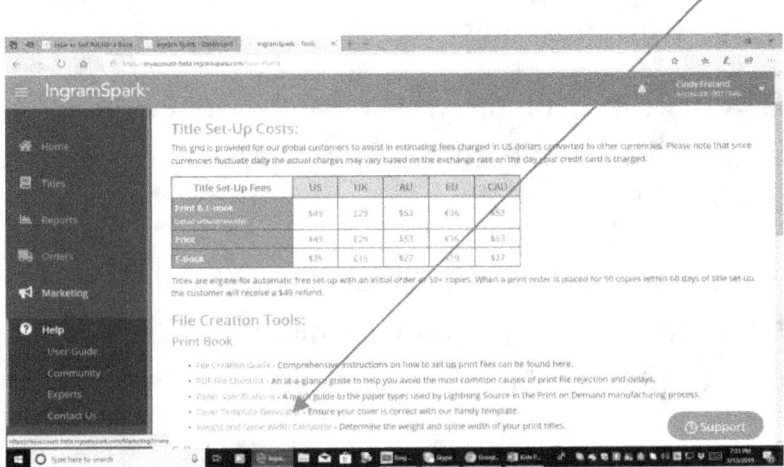

Dashboard

Once you have your account, you can go to Dashboard to:

- add a new title
- find out the status of a new book
- revise books
- order copies of your books
- get a royalties report
- view messages

If you are ever on the website and you need to get back to the dashboard just click "Dashboard" on the top left.

Your name and your member ID are located on the top right. You may need your member ID if you ever need to contact customer service.

Add New Title

To add a new book, just click "Add a New Title." Navigate by clicking any of the links on the left.

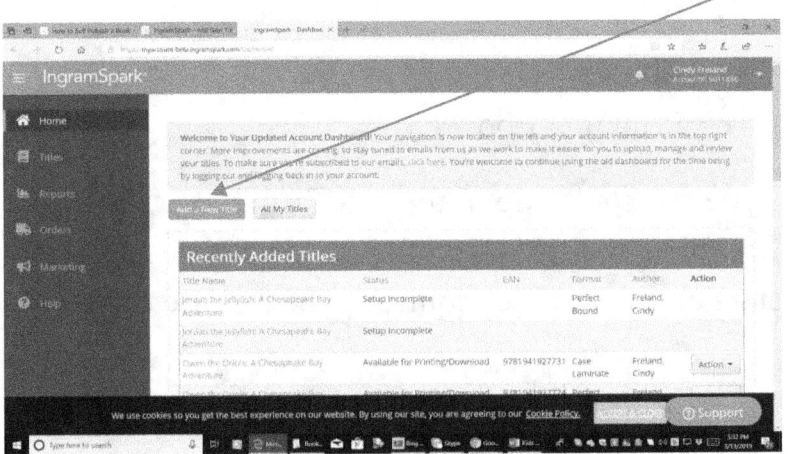

Start Your New Book

By clicking one of the radio buttons under "Choose which type of project you want to start," you can choose:

- Print
- Ebook
- Print and Ebook

Type the book title in the box that reads, "Title." Complete the rest of the boxes. The boxes with red stars on the left are required. The rest are optional.

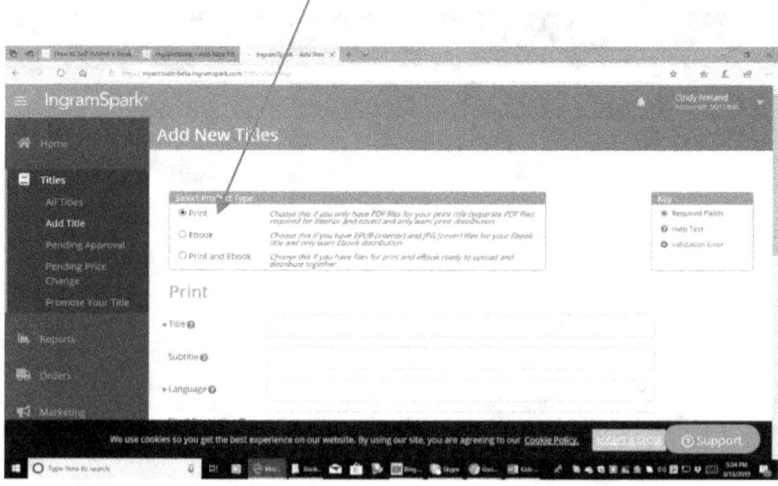

Complete Information

Type in the book details in all boxes. You may click the question marks and arrows for more information.

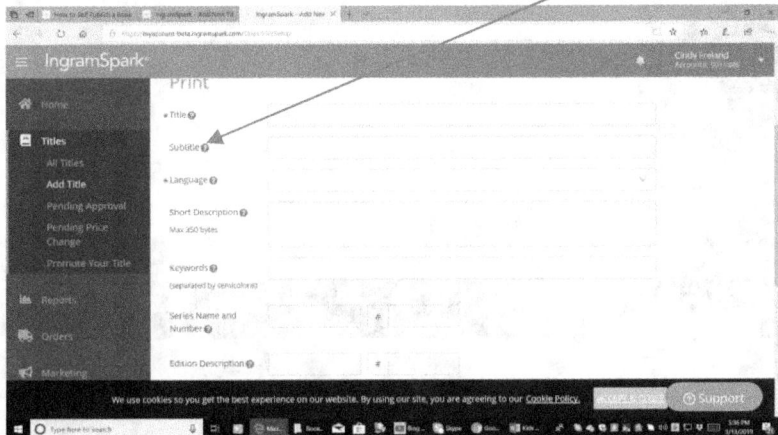

Then click the blue button on the bottom left that reads, "Continue to Step 2 of 5."

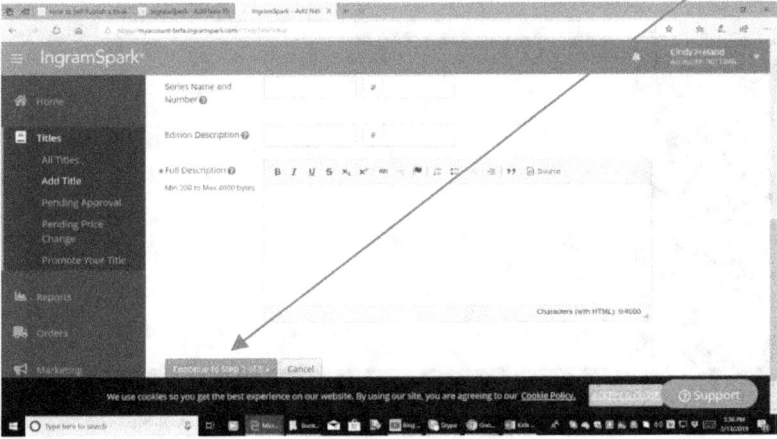

About the Authors/Contributors

Type in the author's and other contributor's names.

Complete Biography, etc.

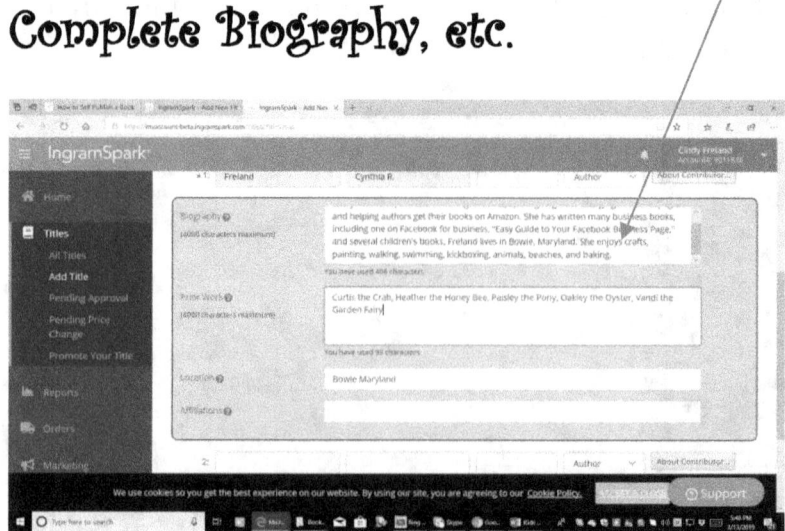

Click the blue button that reads, "Continue to Step 3 of 5."

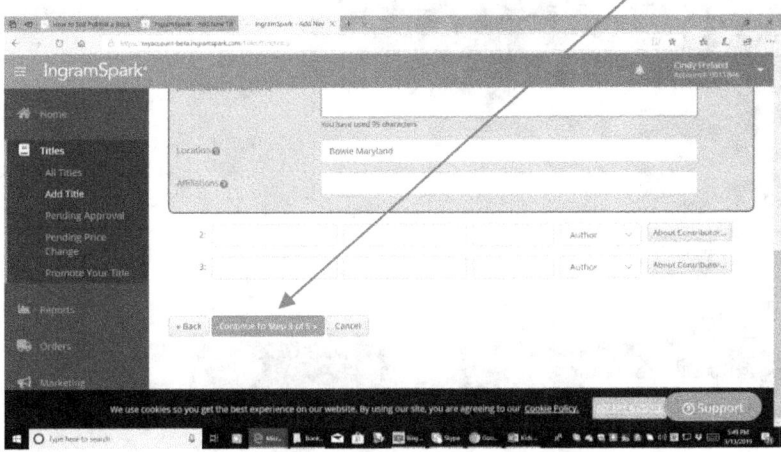

Categorize Your Book

Type the information. You may click on the question marks and boxes that read, "Find Subjects" to get more information.

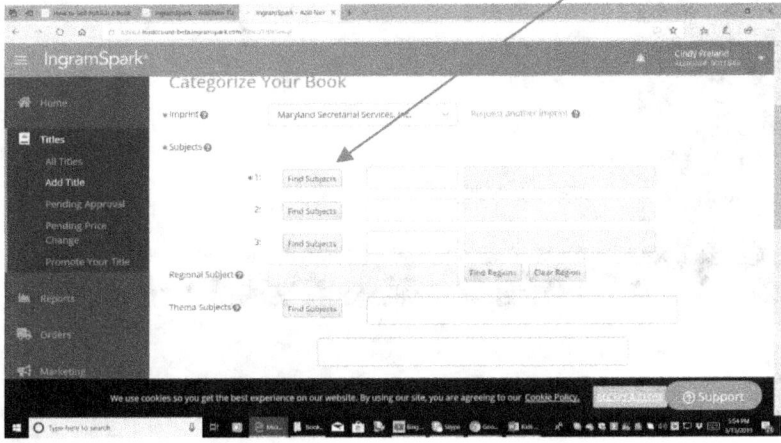

Complete the other boxes.

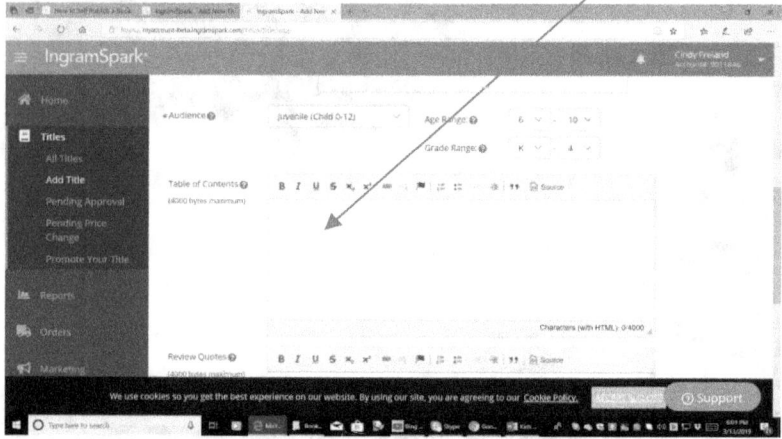

Click the blue button that reads, "Continue to Step 4 of 5."

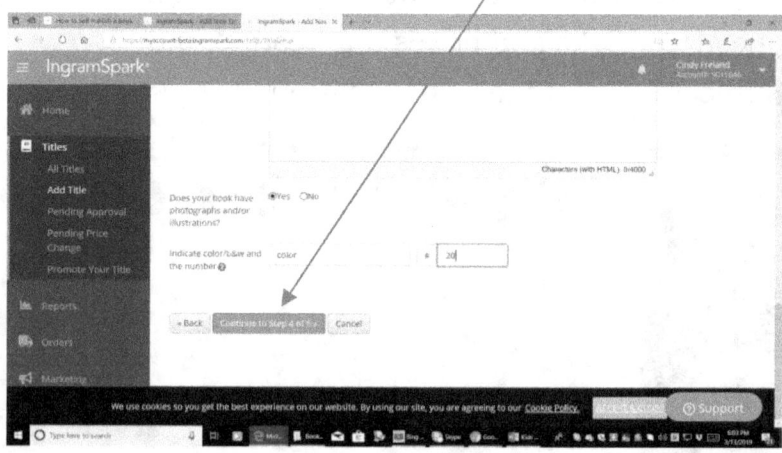

Print Format

Type information into the boxes. Be sure to choose "Premium Color, Color Printed on 70 lb. White Paper" and "Perfect Bound" for best quality for paperbacks. You may also choose hardback from this page as an option.

Perfect Bound is paperback and Case Laminate is hardback.

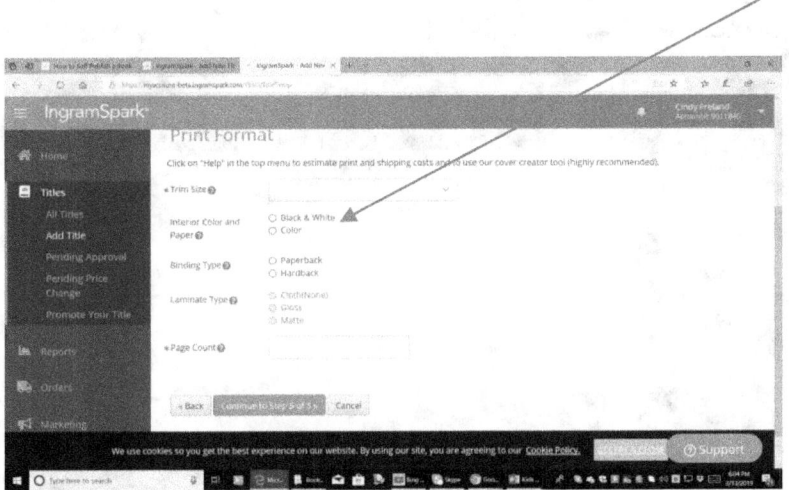

ISBN

The International Standard Book Number (ISBN) is a unique number assigned to each book for commercial sale. You may choose to buy an ISBN from IS or purchase them elsewhere. **You will need a separate ISBN for each format, including ebook, paperback, and hardback, and each vendor who prints your book.**

Type your ISBN and pricing information in these boxes.

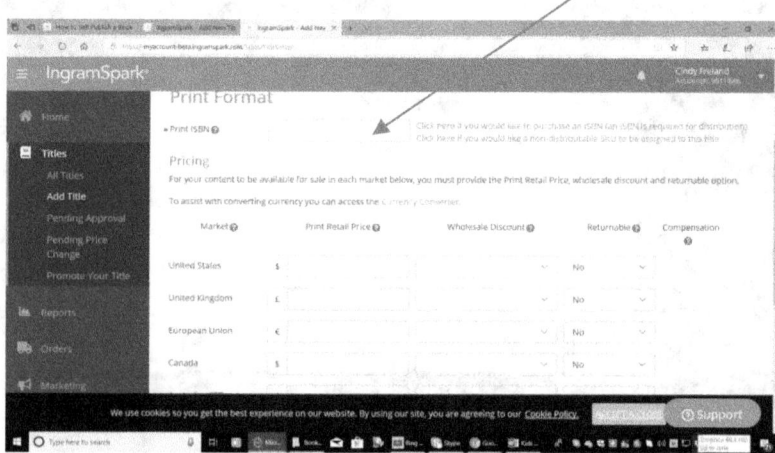

Pricing

Type the information into the boxes. If you are selling to large book stores, be sure you click the "returnable" option.

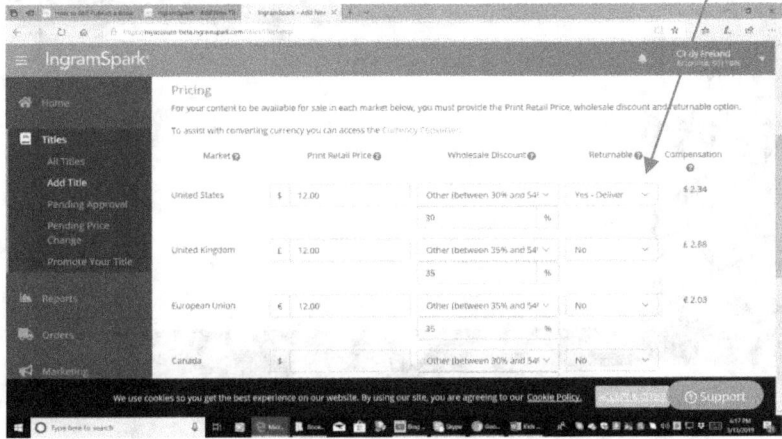

Click the blue button that reads, "Continue."

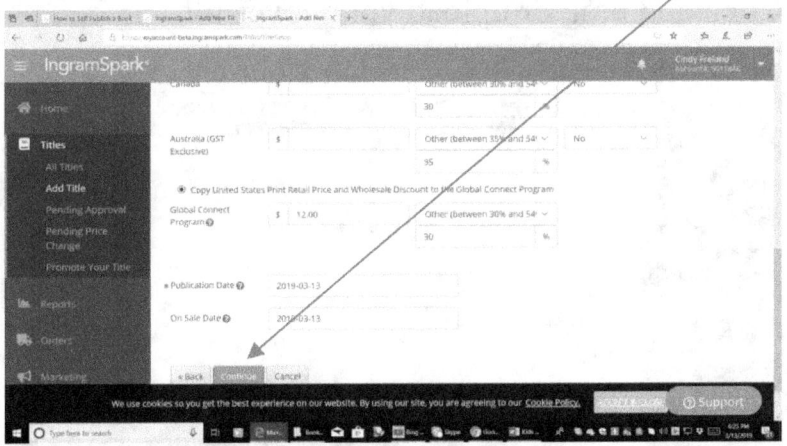

Interior File

You should see your book title at the top. Click and drag or upload your interior file.

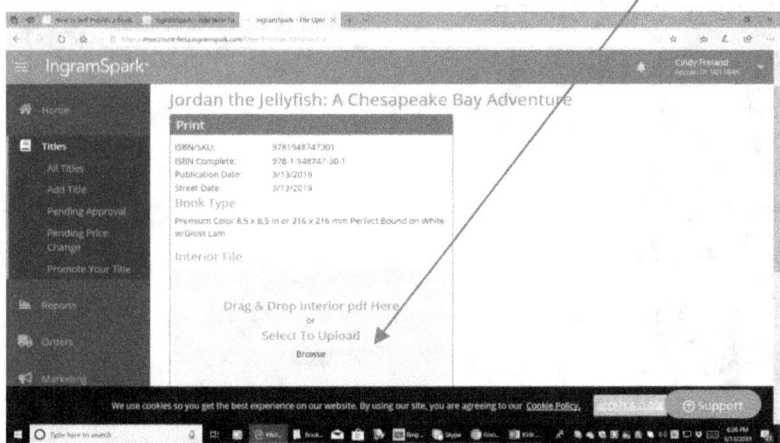

Cover File

Click and drag or upload your cover file.

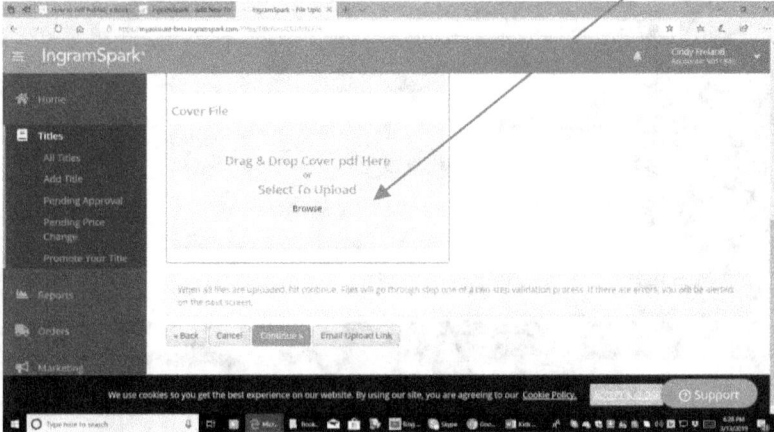

Click the blue button that reads, "Continue."

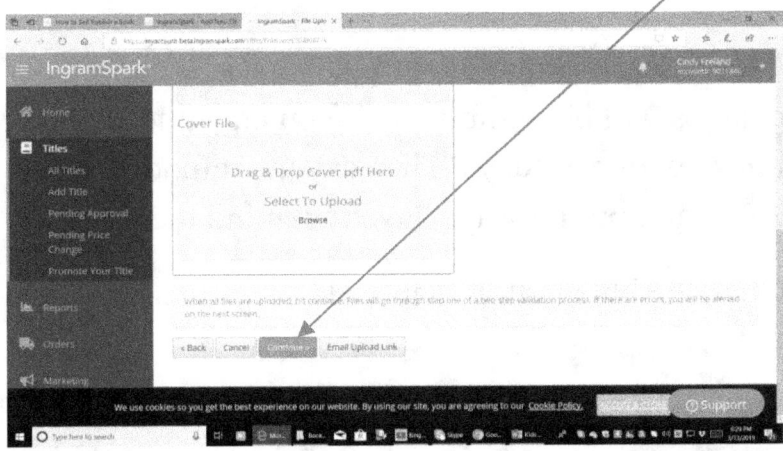

Proceed with Files

Be sure to read these and make corrections as needed. If everything is okay, click the box and "Yes, Proceed with My Files."

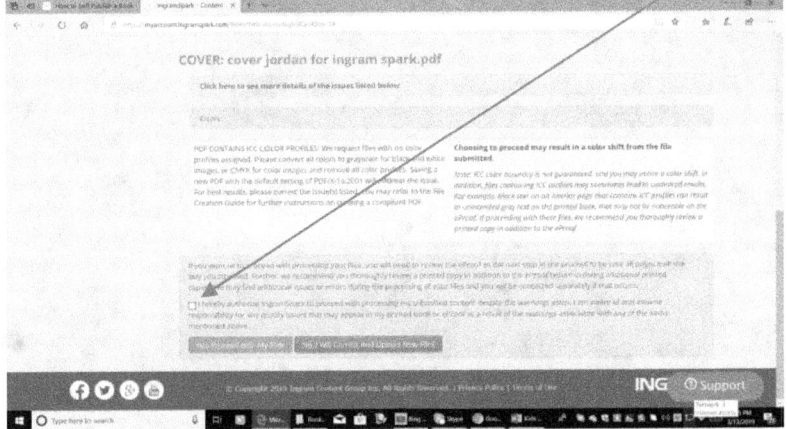

Set Up Charges

Type your information into the boxes. Most charges will be reimbursed if you buy at least 50 books within 30 days. They say the refund is automatic but I always have to remind them.

Click the blue button that reads, "I Agree."

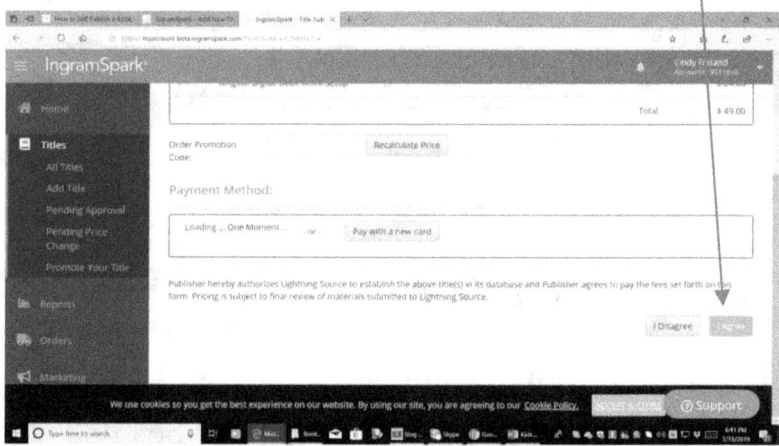

Title Submission Confirmation

If everything went well, you should see this page.

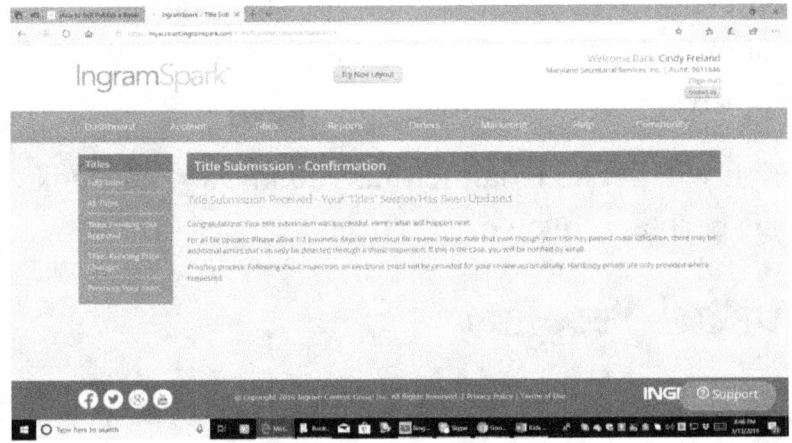

DO NOT PLAGIARIZE! YOU WILL GET CAUGHT AND YOUR BOOK WILL BE REJECTED.

Wait for Approval

When you have revised everything, your cover has been approved and your interior has been submitted, you will wait up to 48 hours for approval.

You will get an email letting you know your book has been approved or you need to revise it.

Digital Proofing

After IS approves your book, they will send you an email or you can check your Dashboard to see the status. Click the link to take you to the page where you will approve the digital image of your book. This will be the final wait time of up to 48 hours to get your book on Amazon.

Preview

Add a preview of your unfinished project or finished works by clicking the "Member Spotlight" tab then "Preview" at the top of the page. Complete four steps to complete the preview.

Purchase Books

You can purchase your own books by clicking "Order Copies." Remember that black and white interiors are the least expensive. My least expensive book costs me only $2.15 plus shipping. There is no minimum for purchase. Books arrive within two weeks.

After you sign in, you will see this page. You may order books here by clicking the blue "order" button.

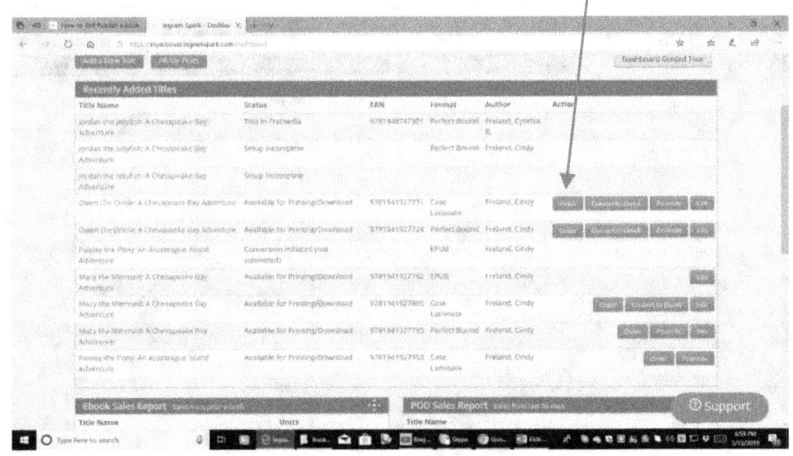

Title Details

If you click on your book title, you will get the details (see details in the second image below).

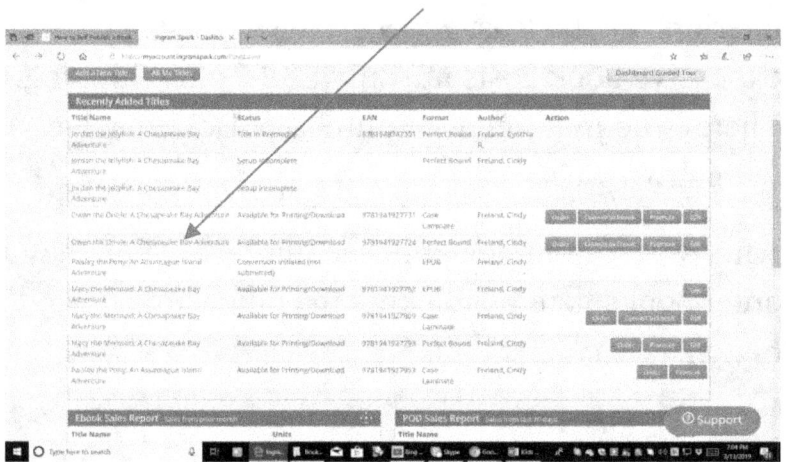

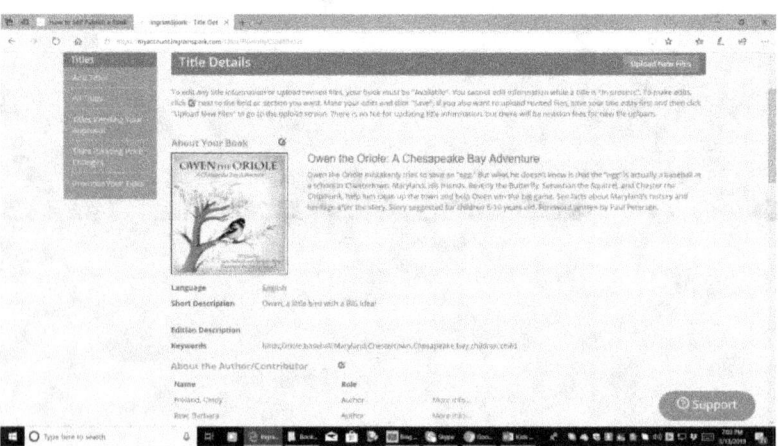

Editing

You can click the book title on your Dashboard and revise any part of your book. If you resubmit the files, you **MAY** have to pay another fee. You might want to check this out by calling or emailing IS BEFORE you resubmit.

Marketing

Once you have your book written, edited, published, and printed, you need to market and sell it. How do you do that? Well, the self-publishing world is not easy. Authors who publish traditionally have marketing staff to help. We, who self-publish, have to do it all ourselves or we have to hire someone to help with marketing. By trial and error I have found a few ways to help sell books. Keep in mind that Amazon will be selling your book as long as it's listed. But I have found that Amazon doesn't sell many of my books because there is so much competition. I have to give it a lot of help.

Stores Sell Your Books

As of the writing of this book (March 20, 2019), my books are available in 55 retail locations and 24 libraries. Since my books are about the animals of the Chesapeake Bay, I searched online and found gift shops, book stores, marinas, museums, and restaurants located around the Bay. I contacted them by liking their Facebook page, sending them a private Facebook message, finding their website, and emailing or calling them. Below is an example of what I wrote to them:

"I have written many children's books about the animals of the Chesapeake Bay. I offer a 40% discount on the $12 paperbacks and 30% off the $18 hardbacks. Are you interested in buying them for your gift shop? You may see book details on my website at www.cbaykidsbooks.com."

Most come back and say, "I would love to offer your books in my store." Some want to buy them and some want to offer them on consignment.

Buying my books mean the store owner or manager orders the books, I ship them or drop them off, and I email or give them an invoice.

Some pay right away if I drop off the books and some will pay the invoice a month or two later. It is all in what you and they agree upon. You must be sure you keep up with them as some will forget to pay. I had some pay three months later.

I keep a paper folder in a file drawer in my desk with the retail location's information. For example, you might want:

Store Name
Contact Name
Address
Phone number
Email address
Orders
Invoices

I paperclip the invoice to the front OUTSIDE of the folder. That way I know they haven't paid. When they pay, I write, "paid (date)" on the invoice and put it INSIDE the folder.

If they want your books on consignment, it means you give them the books and they pay you only after the book sells. They may keep 25-40%, again depending on what you agree upon. They will want you to sign an agreement. Make up a folder for them too.

Every few months, or whenever you decide to check on them, to see if they need more books. They will probably not remember to order from you as they usually order most of their things from larger companies. Your books are not usually on their inventory list.

School Presentations

I love doing school presentations. People who work at schools usually meet me at events. I also email or call schools to ask if they are interested in having me do a presentation. I find the schools in the counties close to the Chesapeake Bay. The presentation consists of me going to the school, talking to the children about keeping the Bay clean and the animals safe, and reading one of my stories. It is usually 30-45 minutes. The largest presentation I did was six in one day to 150 children each for a grand total of 750 children at the same school. I sold $730 in books.

I usually do the presentations at no charge if the school staff emails an order form to the parents. The parents will order books and pay for them in advance. I autograph the books and give them out at the presentations. Some schools offer to pay me $100-350 and I do not turn it down.

Events

I sell the most books at in-person events, such as craft shows, festivals, book signings, and fundraisers. I search for the events online by keying, for example, "events in Bowie, Maryland 2019." You can also find them through social media, including Facebook, LinkedIn, Twitter, Pinterest, and Instagram. We also have a website called Next Door, which is covers very local events. You might also check with friends and family to see if they know any events where you can become a vendor to sell your books.

I usually only have a $50 limit for a vendor fee but sometimes I will pay more. It all depends on the size of the event. Some events draw 10,000 people and those are the ones I am willing to pay more, maybe up to $150.

As people look at my books or walk by, I say, "I am the author of all these books. They are about the animals of the Chesapeake Bay." Some vendors sell other people's books, including Usborne. I want people to know that I am the author. They become curious when they hear that I have written the stories.

Be sure you have plenty of change for the events. Buyers may give you a large bill and you will have to give them change. I usually carry plenty of ones and fives. I use PayPal Now to accept credit cards on my Windows cell phone. PayPal charges me $30 plus and small transaction fee. It goes into my checking account within 48 hours. You may also use Square on your cell phone.

I use a white table cover with a colorful table runner. The runner matches my 5' banner that stands beside or behind my table. I have a black, metal folding display rack to hold my books. I place several hardback books beside the rack with several stuffed animals that match my Bay books. I always leave space in the back of the table for me to autograph books. I keep a tally of the books I sell. I keep the books clean and dry by hauling them in a rolling cooler.

If you have a smaller vehicle, like my Chevy Spark, you may still be able to fit everything. I fold down the rear seats and fit two card tables, folding chair, canopy, display rack, rolling shopping cart, cooler, two tote bags, and banner. Inside events usually provide a table and chair and you won't need your canopy. Check the vendor application to see if you need to bring a table, chair, and canopy.

Below is a photo of my table with the canopy at an outside event.

Below is a photo of my table with my banner and table runner at an inside event.

Contact Me

Visit my website at www.marylandsecretarial.com www.cbaykidsbooks.com or email me at cindy@marylandsecretarial.com or call (301) 352-7927. Like me on Facebook at www.facebook.com/cindyfrelandauthor. You can also find me on LinkedIn, Twitter and YouTube.

Also check out the children's and business books written by Cindy Freland on Amazon.com.

Books Written by Cindy Freland

available on Amazon.com and ww.cbaykidsbooks.com:

Jordan the Jellyfish: A Chesapeake Bay Adventure
Curtis the Crab: A Chesapeake Bay Adventure
Heather the Honey Bee: A Chesapeake Bay Adventure
Oakley the Oyster: A Chesapeake Bay Adventure
Olivia the Osprey: A Chesapeake Bay Adventure
Owen the Oriole: A Chesapeake Bay Adventure
Chester the Chipmunk: A Chesapeake Bay Adventure
Christmas with Marco: A Chesapeake Bay Adventure
Macy the Mermaid: A Chesapeake Bay Adventure
Lila the Ladybug: A Deep Creek Lake Adventure
Paisley the Pony: An Assateague Island Adventure
Vandi the Garden Fairy
Mud Pies

Author: Cindy Freland

Cindy Freland's inspiration comes from her love of children and animals. Most of her children's books are based on true events. She founded Maryland Secretarial Services, Inc. in 1997. She has won three business awards and teaches business workshops at two local community colleges, a senior center and two chamber of commerce offices. She has written many business books, including one on Facebook for business, "Easy Guide to Your Facebook Business Page," and several children's books. You can find her children's books about the Chesapeake Bay on www.cbaykidsbooks.com and all the others on www.amazon.com. Freland lives in Bowie, Maryland.

Dedicated to my

beloved daughters,

Alyssa Thomas, Andrea Bean,

and my precious granddaughter,
Cambria

Thanks for all your support,
confidence, smiles, and love.

www.ingramcontent.com/pod-product-compliance
Lightning Source LLC
Chambersburg PA
CBHW052210110526
44591CB00012B/2153